TREE
pages 30 and 31

D1543143

GENOME
pages 18 and 19

G G A T T A A G G C

GENE
pages 14, 15, 16 and 17

B E R I N G I A
pages 40 and 41

MICE AND LICE
pages 46 and 47

NORTH

AMERICA
pages 40 and

TRAINS, PLANES
AND AUTOMOBILES
pages 46 and 47

SOUTH PACIFIC
pages 42 and 43

HOMO SAPIENS
pages 4, 5, 10
and 11

CHROMOSOME
pages 15, 28
and 29

SOUTH

AMERICA
pages 40 and
41

Monte Verde
pages 13 and 41

X CHROMOSOME
pages 26 and 27

DNA
pages 14- 25, 30, 31 and 42

Around the World in 22 Million Days

The Great Human Journey

Ian Tattersall, Rob DeSalle, and Patricia J. Wynne

THE ADVENTURES of THE MUSEUM MICE

with Wallace and Darwin,
the Museum Mice

Are you ready? Let's go.

Bunker Hill Publishing

Hi! I'm Wallace.

I'm Darwin.

Homo sapiens—All Over the Planet

Today, our species, *Homo sapiens,* is found in almost every environment the world has to offer, year-round—even at the South Pole! From the world's great deserts—the Sahara, the Gobi, the Kalahari—to the great rain forests of the Amazon basin and Southeast Asia, people have found ways of living everywhere. Most people manage this today by settling down and cultivating the earth and raising animals; but sometimes accommodating to particularly difficult environments—such as those deserts and forests—still means lifestyles spent on the move, much like our early ancestors. No other creature is able to make a living in so many different kinds of habitat.

And the way humans manage this is through culture. Unlike other animals, humans today do not adapt physically to local conditions. Instead, they manage to accommodate to the environments around them through their technologies. They put up tents to give shade in the deserts, and build well-insulated houses that can be heated in the bitter northern winters. They dig wells to find water where there is none on the surface, and they boil roots to get rid of poisons. It is this mental and technological complexity, not their physical features, that is the secret of their success.

We're the museum mice. We live in the American Museum of Natural History. This is an anthropology hall. You must be wondering why we are here.

Hey Darwin! Check out these tiny bipeds from more than three million years ago!

Looking Back in Time

The people who try to figure out how human beings came to take over the entire Earth are called paleoanthropologists. These are the folk who look for the remains and artifacts of ancient humans across the globe and use them to reconstruct the story of human evolution.

Some paleoanthropologists study fossils. Human fossils are the petrified remains of our ancient relatives, called hominids, and they show that in the past there were typically lots of different hominids around. That's very different from today, when *Homo sapiens* is the only hominid in the world. Being alone in the world makes us think that there was always just one kind of hominid at any one time, but the fossils show it just wasn't so.

Some paleoanthropologists are archaeologists. These scientists study how human technologies and cultures have evolved. Interestingly, this doesn't seem to have been in step with human physical evolution. Technologies have always been invented by species that were already there!

Yes, these were the first kind of hominid. They had small bodies and brains, they probably spent some time in the trees, and they all lived in Africa.

Wow, we've come a long way! It's hot here!

But it was worth it. Here we are in the birthplace of mankind. Although I'm a mouse I'm still getting a kind of shivery feeling.

And it's only the beginning of our journey.

1.8-million-year-old tool and flakes from Olduvai Gorge

Paranthropus found near the stone tools

Modern Humans

Africa was the place where human ancestors, those ancient hominids, first evolved. For several million years hominids only lived in Africa, where certain species eventually got taller bodies and bigger brains. About two million years ago, ancient humans first traveled out of Africa. Soon they had journeyed east to Java and China, and by over a million years ago their descendants had also gotten into Europe, where they eventually gave rise to *Homo neanderthalensis*. But some of them stayed behind in Africa, and these stay-at-home hominids evolved into our species, *Homo sapiens*.

Today, there are billions of *Homo sapiens* in the world. But at first there was only a tiny population of them, probably somewhere in eastern Africa. These people looked just like people today, but they behaved much as their ancestors did. Then something happened that made them start thinking differently about themselves and the world around them. From that point, the tiny population started behaving in a new way. Its members started speaking, and imagining how the world might be, instead of just reacting to things happening around them. And shortly after this, the new kind of human being started spreading out of Africa.

That's because the story of how humans took over the world is a long one.

And it is told not only by artifacts and fossils, but also by DNA. But let's start with archaeology.

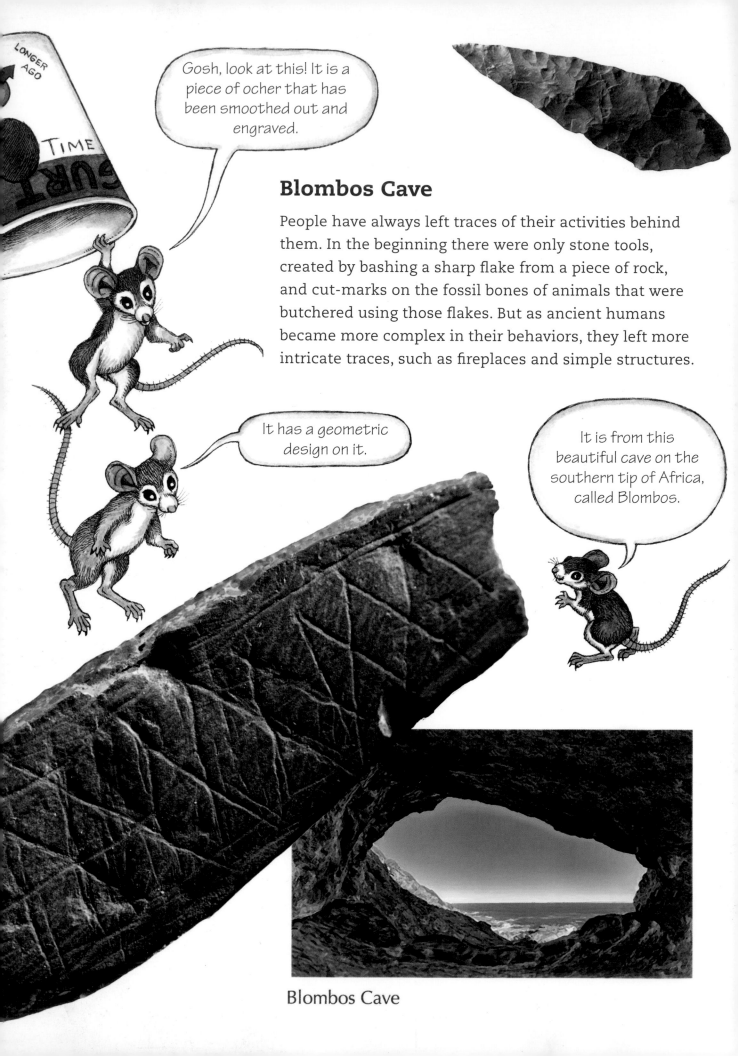

Gosh, look at this! It is a piece of ocher that has been smoothed out and engraved.

Blombos Cave

People have always left traces of their activities behind them. In the beginning there were only stone tools, created by bashing a sharp flake from a piece of rock, and cut-marks on the fossil bones of animals that were butchered using those flakes. But as ancient humans became more complex in their behaviors, they left more intricate traces, such as fireplaces and simple structures.

It has a geometric design on it.

It is from this beautiful cave on the southern tip of Africa, called Blombos.

Blombos Cave

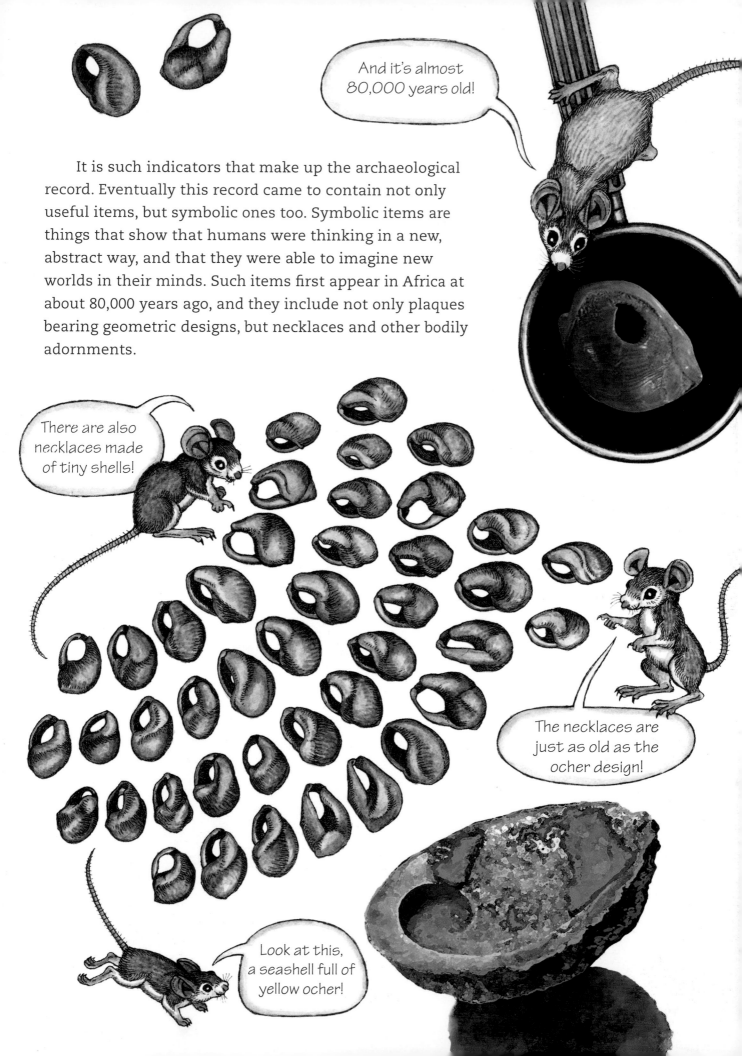

And it's almost 80,000 years old!

It is such indicators that make up the archaeological record. Eventually this record came to contain not only useful items, but symbolic ones too. Symbolic items are things that show that humans were thinking in a new, abstract way, and that they were able to imagine new worlds in their minds. Such items first appear in Africa at about 80,000 years ago, and they include not only plaques bearing geometric designs, but necklaces and other bodily adornments.

There are also necklaces made of tiny shells!

The necklaces are just as old as the ocher design!

Look at this, a seashell full of yellow ocher!

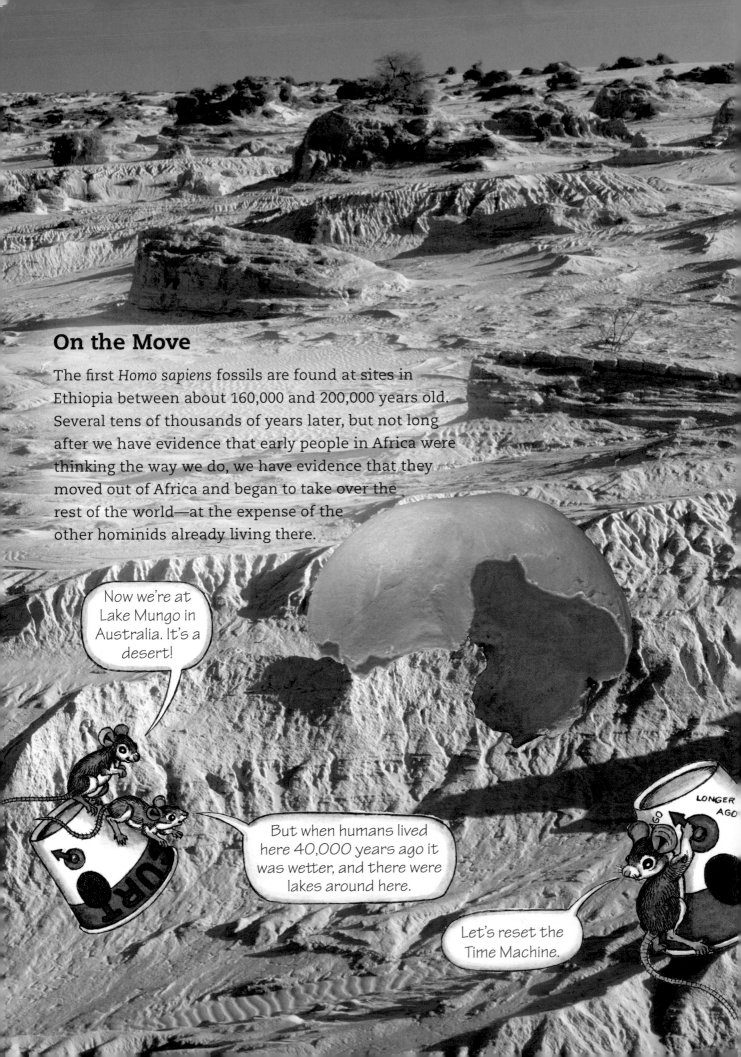

On the Move

The first *Homo sapiens* fossils are found at sites in
Ethiopia between about 160,000 and 200,000 years old.
Several tens of thousands of years later, but not long
after we have evidence that early people in Africa were
thinking the way we do, we have evidence that they
moved out of Africa and began to take over the
rest of the world—at the expense of the
other hominids already living there.

Now we're at
Lake Mungo in
Australia. It's a
desert!

But when humans lived
here 40,000 years ago it
was wetter, and there were
lakes around here.

Let's reset the
Time Machine.

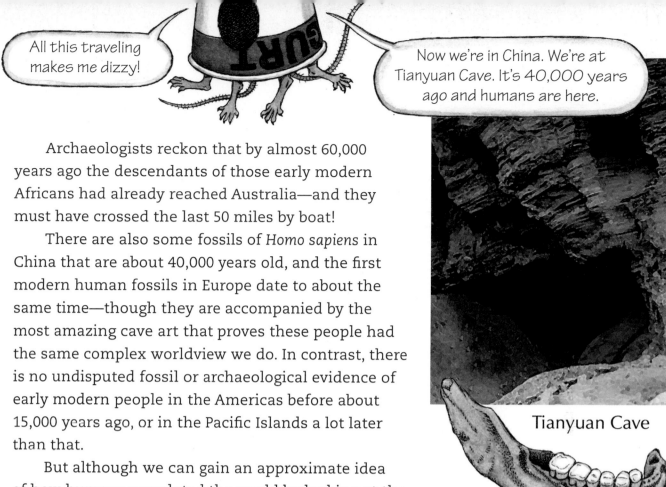

All this traveling makes me dizzy!

Now we're in China. We're at Tianyuan Cave. It's 40,000 years ago and humans are here.

Archaeologists reckon that by almost 60,000 years ago the descendants of those early modern Africans had already reached Australia—and they must have crossed the last 50 miles by boat!

There are also some fossils of *Homo sapiens* in China that are about 40,000 years old, and the first modern human fossils in Europe date to about the same time—though they are accompanied by the most amazing cave art that proves these people had the same complex worldview we do. In contrast, there is no undisputed fossil or archaeological evidence of early modern people in the Americas before about 15,000 years ago, or in the Pacific Islands a lot later than that.

But although we can gain an approximate idea of how humans populated the world by looking at the fossils and artifacts they left behind, we have a much more powerful tool at our disposal—our DNA!

Tianyuan Cave

Back to the Time Machine!

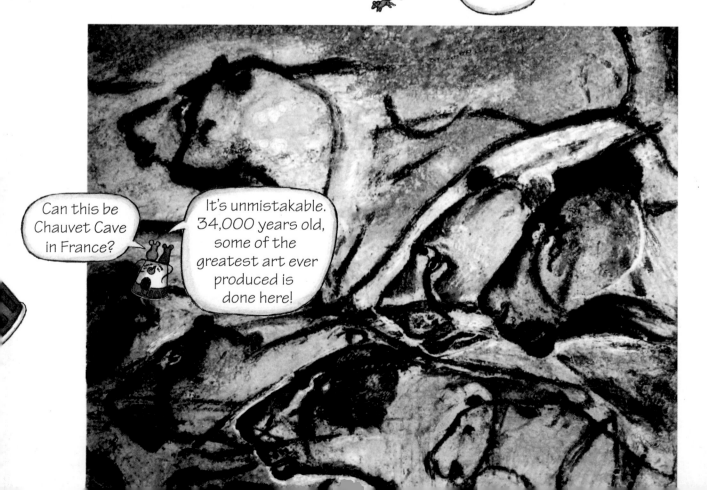

Can this be Chauvet Cave in France?

It's unmistakable. 34,000 years old, some of the greatest art ever produced is done here!

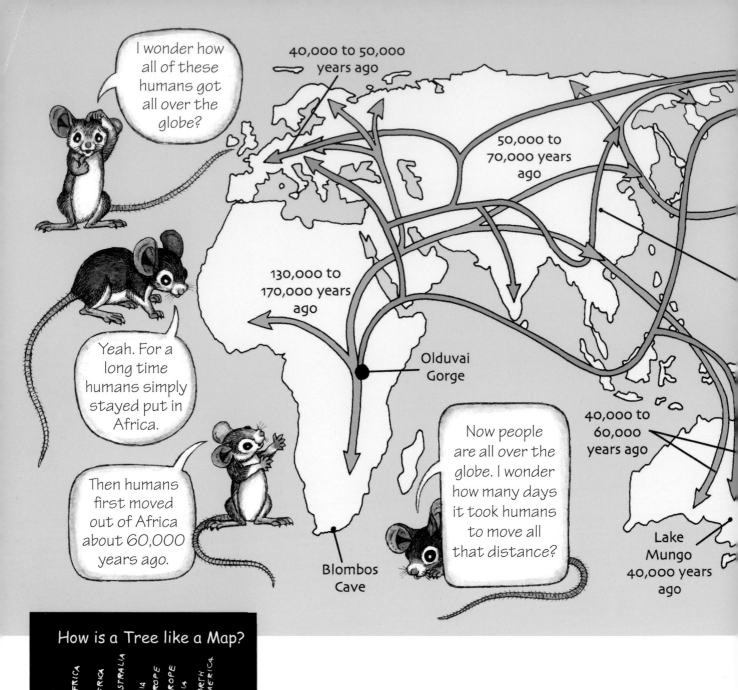

Around the World in 22 Million Days

DNA can give us information on how the mitochondria of women and the Y chromosomes of men are related to each other. The information is placed into a branching diagram called a tree. A tree for mitochondria is generated separately from a tree for the Y chromosome. The tips of the tree are the mitochondrial DNA (mtDNA) and the Y chromosome DNA from living people. If the first branch on the mtDNA tree has a lot of mitochondrial DNA from aboriginal people from Australia then this means the

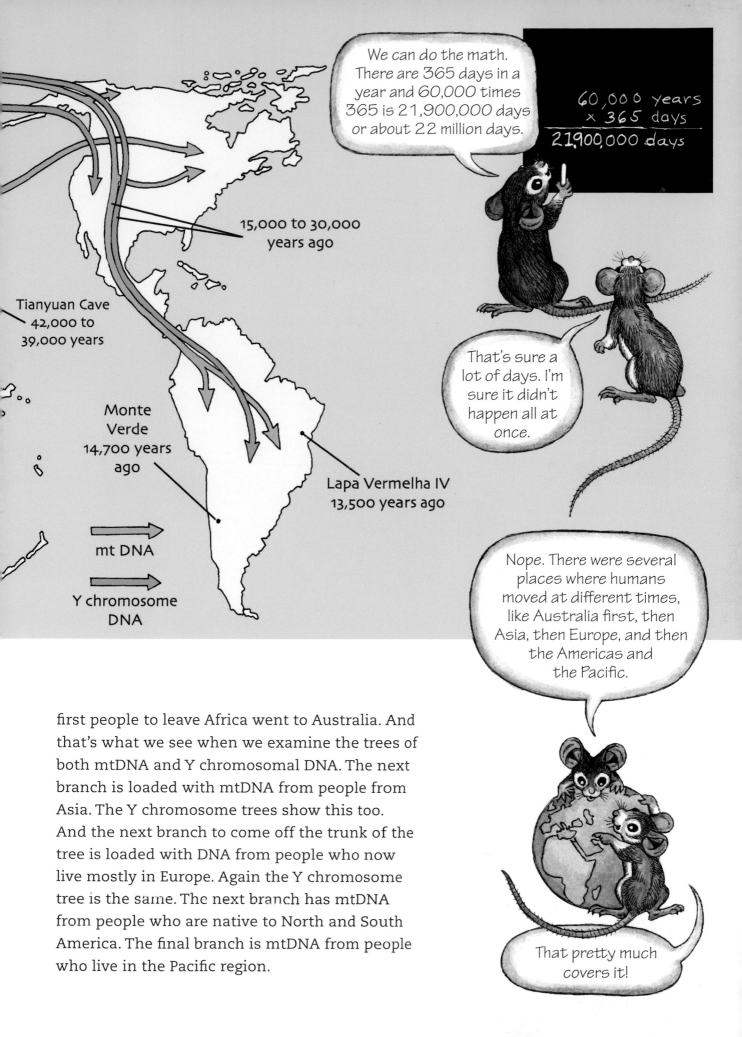

We can do the math. There are 365 days in a year and 60,000 times 365 is 21,900,000 days or about 22 million days.

60,000 years
× 365 days
21,900,000 days

15,000 to 30,000 years ago

Tianyuan Cave 42,000 to 39,000 years

Monte Verde 14,700 years ago

Lapa Vermelha IV 13,500 years ago

mt DNA

Y chromosome DNA

That's sure a lot of days. I'm sure it didn't happen all at once.

Nope. There were several places where humans moved at different times, like Australia first, then Asia, then Europe, and then the Americas and the Pacific.

first people to leave Africa went to Australia. And that's what we see when we examine the trees of both mtDNA and Y chromosomal DNA. The next branch is loaded with mtDNA from people from Asia. The Y chromosome trees show this too. And the next branch to come off the trunk of the tree is loaded with DNA from people who now live mostly in Europe. Again the Y chromosome tree is the same. The next branch has mtDNA from people who are native to North and South America. The final branch is mtDNA from people who live in the Pacific region.

That pretty much covers it!

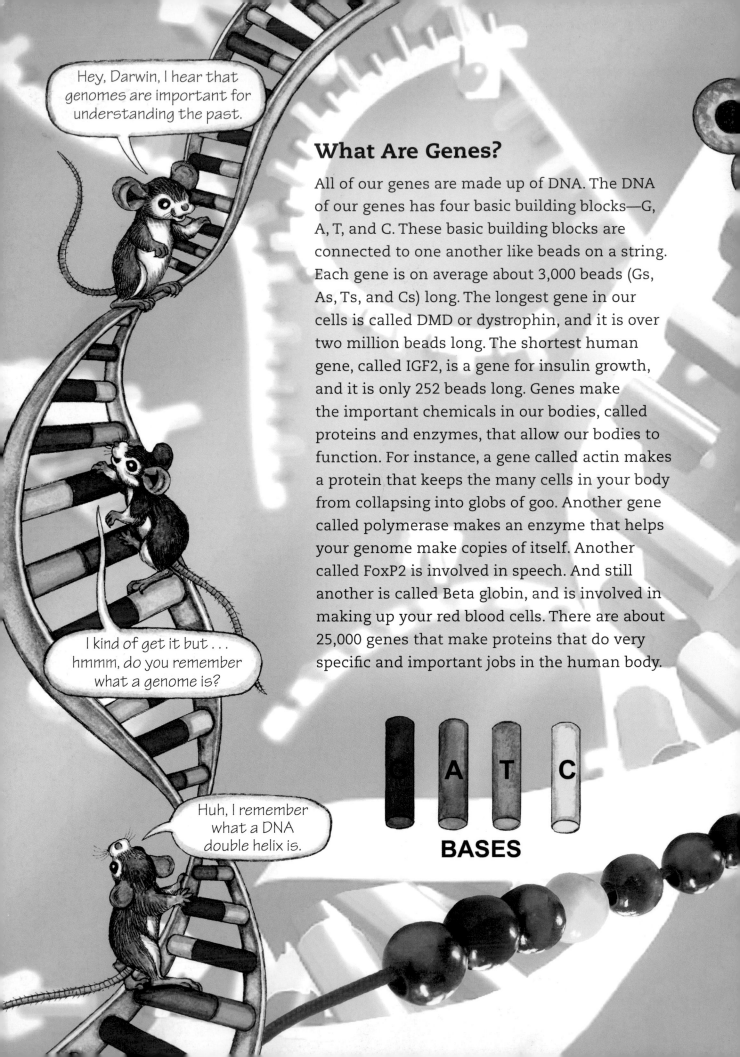

Hey, Darwin, I hear that genomes are important for understanding the past.

I kind of get it but . . . hmmm, do you remember what a genome is?

Huh, I remember what a DNA double helix is.

What Are Genes?

All of our genes are made up of DNA. The DNA of our genes has four basic building blocks—G, A, T, and C. These basic building blocks are connected to one another like beads on a string. Each gene is on average about 3,000 beads (Gs, As, Ts, and Cs) long. The longest gene in our cells is called DMD or dystrophin, and it is over two million beads long. The shortest human gene, called IGF2, is a gene for insulin growth, and it is only 252 beads long. Genes make the important chemicals in our bodies, called proteins and enzymes, that allow our bodies to function. For instance, a gene called actin makes a protein that keeps the many cells in your body from collapsing into globs of goo. Another gene called polymerase makes an enzyme that helps your genome make copies of itself. Another called FoxP2 is involved in speech. And still another is called Beta globin, and is involved in making up your red blood cells. There are about 25,000 genes that make proteins that do very specific and important jobs in the human body.

G A T C

BASES

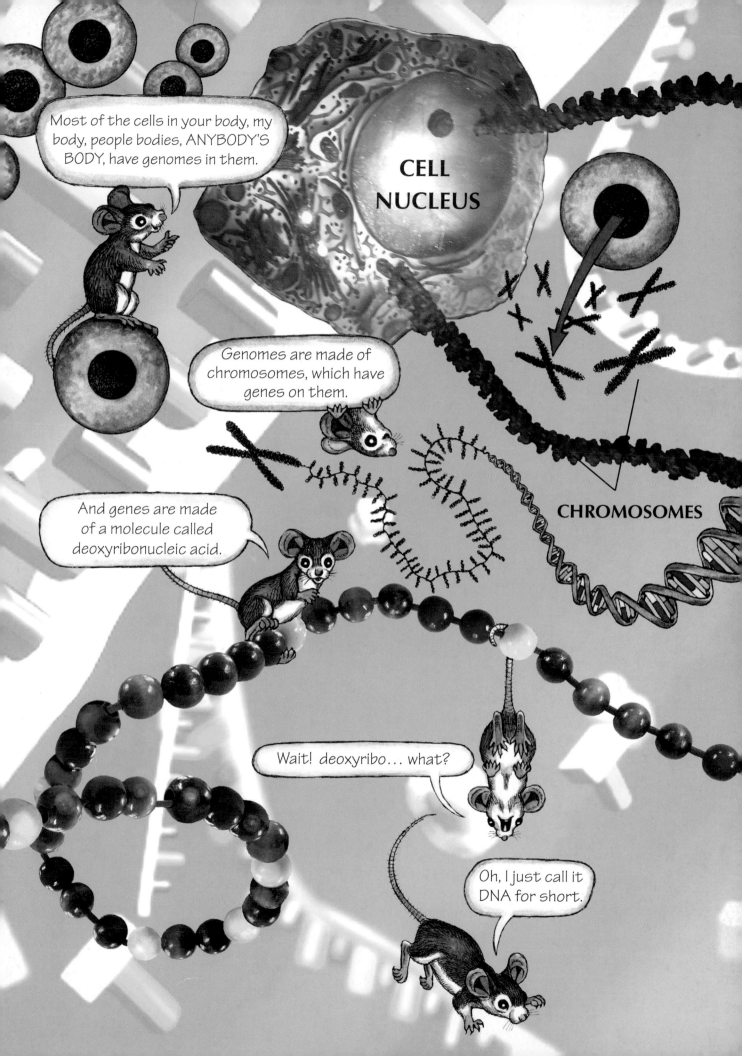

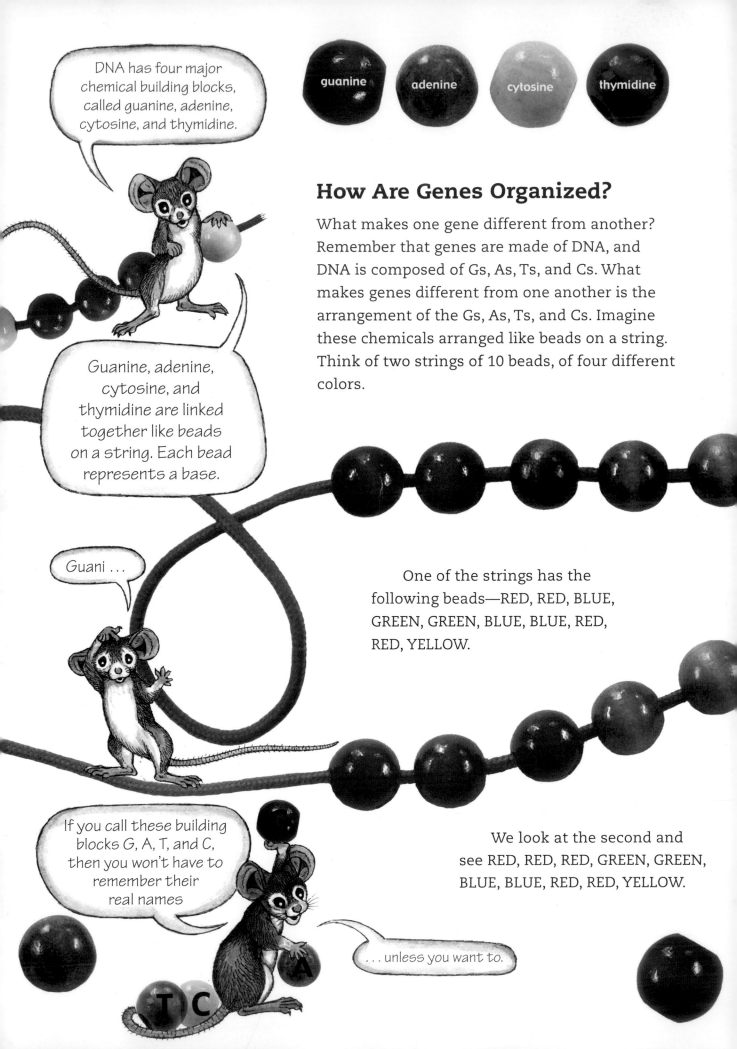

How Are Genes Organized?

What makes one gene different from another? Remember that genes are made of DNA, and DNA is composed of Gs, As, Ts, and Cs. What makes genes different from one another is the arrangement of the Gs, As, Ts, and Cs. Imagine these chemicals arranged like beads on a string. Think of two strings of 10 beads, of four different colors.

One of the strings has the following beads—RED, RED, BLUE, GREEN, GREEN, BLUE, BLUE, RED, RED, YELLOW.

We look at the second and see RED, RED, RED, GREEN, GREEN, BLUE, BLUE, RED, RED, YELLOW.

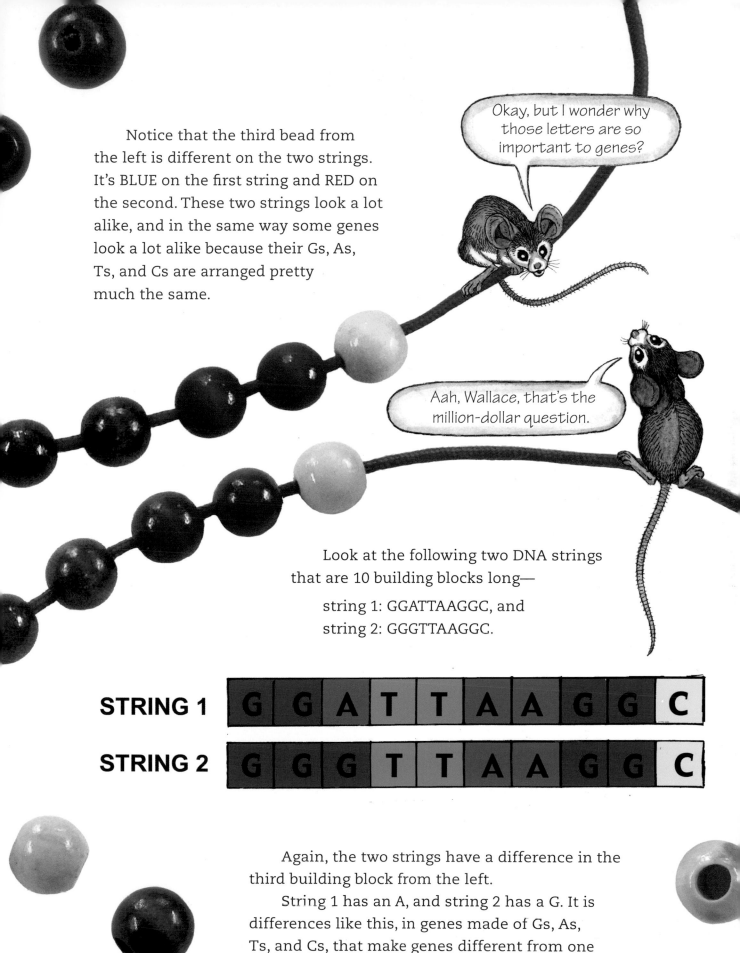

Notice that the third bead from the left is different on the two strings. It's BLUE on the first string and RED on the second. These two strings look a lot alike, and in the same way some genes look a lot alike because their Gs, As, Ts, and Cs are arranged pretty much the same.

Okay, but I wonder why those letters are so important to genes?

Aah, Wallace, that's the million-dollar question.

Look at the following two DNA strings that are 10 building blocks long—

string 1: GGATTAAGGC, and
string 2: GGGTTAAGGC.

STRING 1	G	G	A	T	T	A	A	G	G	C
STRING 2	G	G	G	T	T	A	A	G	G	C

Again, the two strings have a difference in the third building block from the left.

String 1 has an A, and string 2 has a G. It is differences like this, in genes made of Gs, As, Ts, and Cs, that make genes different from one another.

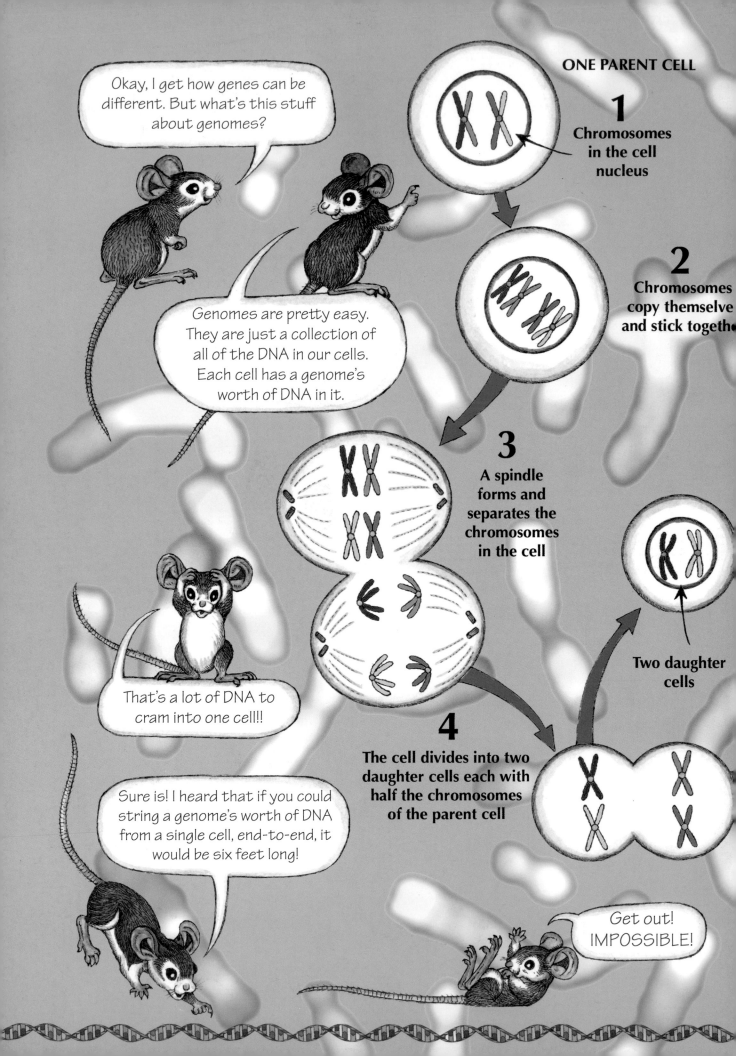

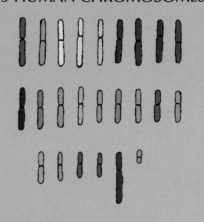

What Is a Genome?

Each of us gets a genome's worth of DNA from our mother, and a genome's worth from our father. There are some exceptions, such as mtDNA and Y chromosomes, that we will look at in the following pages. How does this happen? Does this mean that my genome is twice as big as my parents' genome? Remember that your mom's genome has two copies, one from her mom (your grandma) and one from her dad (your grandpa). So when your mom makes eggs her body produces the eggs with only one half of the DNA from her genome. Her eggs have all of the genes needed to make a fertile egg. Your father's sperm is made the same way. So when a mom's egg and a dad's sperm come together to produce an embryo, the genomes don't get bigger. They just stay the same size as the genomes in their parents' cells.

7
New cells with one half the parent cell's genome are formed

5
Spindles form again

6 Cells divide

It IS possible. DNA is super-compressed into things called chromosomes.

Wow! Four new eggs, or four new sperm.

3 billion GATCs and 1 copy of each gene

EGG
(MOTHER'S CELL)

SPERM CELL
(FATHER'S CELL)

3 billion GATCS and
1 copy of each gene

How Are Genomes Inherited?

A full genome of a human has six billion G, A, T, and Cs, and two copies of each gene in it. A sperm has three billion G, A, T, and Cs, and only one copy of each gene in it. Likewise for the egg. These three billion GATCs code for about 25,000 genes. Each of these genes has a unique history because it comes from different people or places. That is, they all come from the many different ancestors you have. On average, you will share half of your DNA with your parents. And then one quarter of your DNA with your grandparents.

Species can have different numbers of chromosomes. Our species is *Mus musculus*, and WE have 20 pairs of chromosomes.

How many chromosomes do we mice have??

Darn! Not as many as humans!

MOUSE
CHROMOSOMES

Y

X

OFFSPRING'S CELL

6 billion GATCs and 2 copies of each gene

Amount of DNA from your parents

And then one eighth of your DNA with your great-grandparents. And then one sixteenth of your DNA with your great-great-grandparents. By the time you look at your great-great-great-great-great-great-great-great-grandparents (someone who might have lived 300 years ago) you should share less than 1 percent of your DNA with them. This is just slightly more than the same amount of DNA you would share on average with someone who is not related to you, who is randomly chosen from a crowd.

Amount of DNA from your grandparents

Amount of DNA from your great-grandparents

Yeah, but while we have fewer chromosomes, we have just about the same number of genes!!

25,000 GENES HUMAN

25,000 GENES MOUSE

Well, that's okay then, I guess, Darwin.

Amount of DNA from your great-great-grandparents

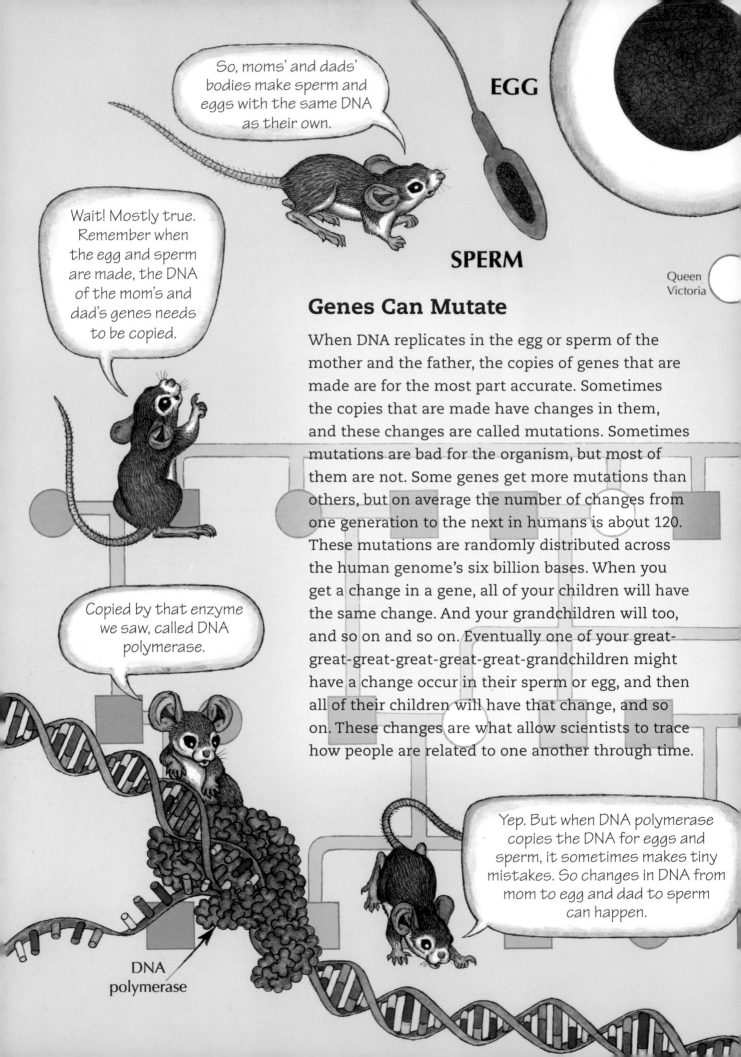

So, moms' and dads' bodies make sperm and eggs with the same DNA as their own.

EGG

SPERM

Wait! Mostly true. Remember when the egg and sperm are made, the DNA of the mom's and dad's genes needs to be copied.

Queen Victoria

Genes Can Mutate

When DNA replicates in the egg or sperm of the mother and the father, the copies of genes that are made are for the most part accurate. Sometimes the copies that are made have changes in them, and these changes are called mutations. Sometimes mutations are bad for the organism, but most of them are not. Some genes get more mutations than others, but on average the number of changes from one generation to the next in humans is about 120. These mutations are randomly distributed across the human genome's six billion bases. When you get a change in a gene, all of your children will have the same change. And your grandchildren will too, and so on and so on. Eventually one of your great-great-great-great-great-great-grandchildren might have a change occur in their sperm or egg, and then all of their children will have that change, and so on. These changes are what allow scientists to trace how people are related to one another through time.

Copied by that enzyme we saw, called DNA polymerase.

Yep. But when DNA polymerase copies the DNA for eggs and sperm, it sometimes makes tiny mistakes. So changes in DNA from mom to egg and dad to sperm can happen.

DNA polymerase

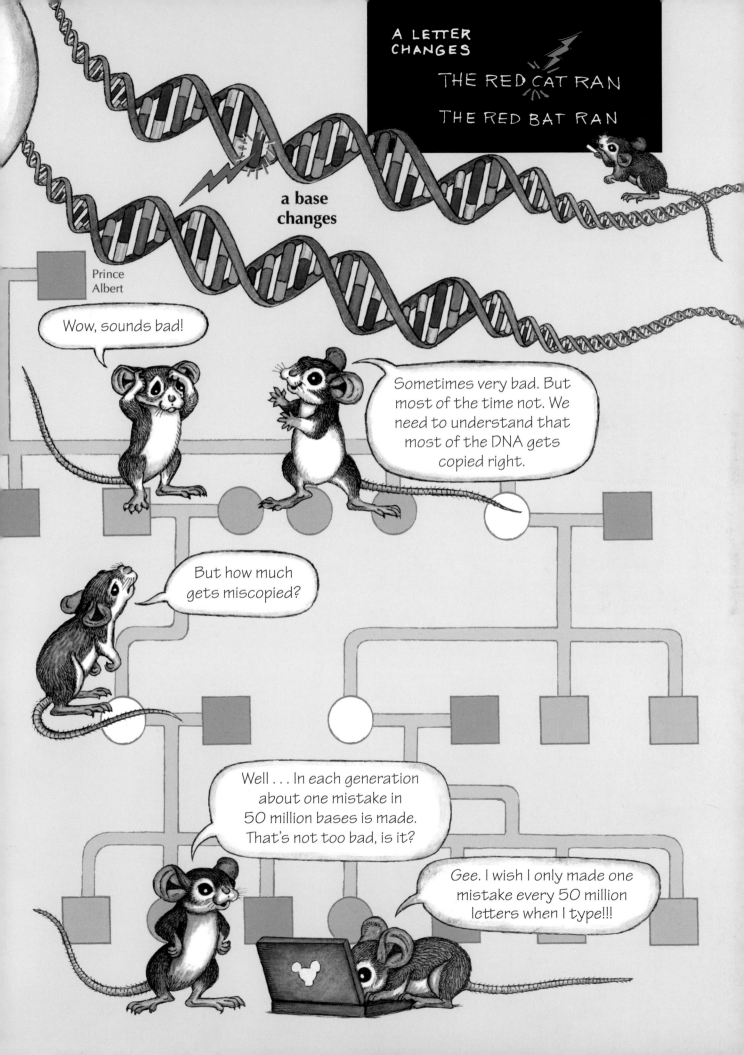

ANIMAL CELL

MITOCH

Following Female Footsteps

Mitochondria are the powerhouses of the cell. They take oxygen breathed into the body, and absorbed by the cell, transforming it into energy. Each and every one of the millions of mitochondria in your body has a small circular piece of DNA in it called a mitochondrial genome. This small genome in animals has only about 13 genes that code for proteins. The genome is only a little over 10,000 Gs, As, Ts, and Cs long. This is only about 1/100,000 of the entire DNA of a cell.

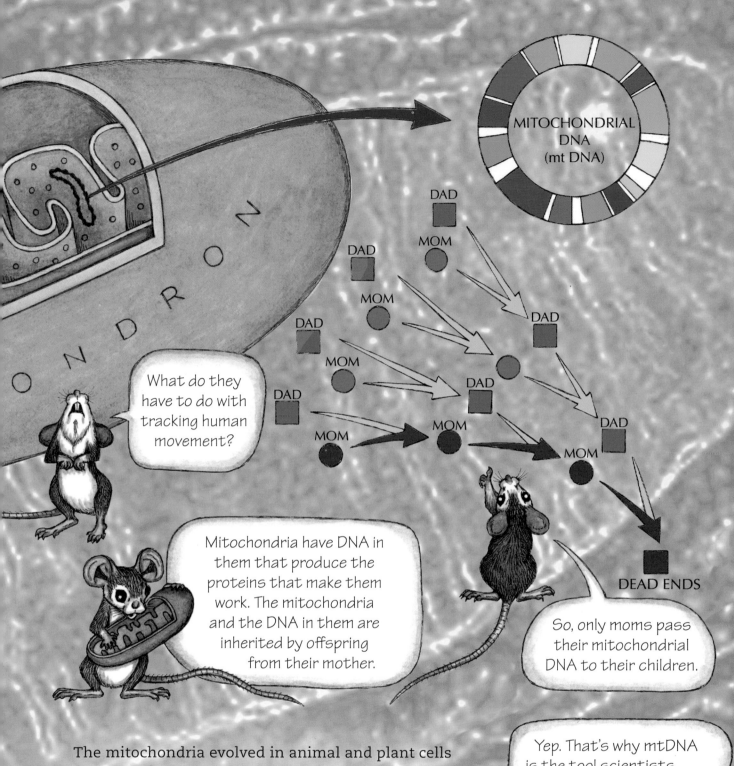

MITOCHONDRIAL DNA (mt DNA)

What do they have to do with tracking human movement?

Mitochondria have DNA in them that produce the proteins that make them work. The mitochondria and the DNA in them are inherited by offspring from their mother.

DAD
MOM

DEAD ENDS

So, only moms pass their mitochondrial DNA to their children.

The mitochondria evolved in animal and plant cells as a result of an ancient event when an ancestral cell swallowed a bacteria, and kept it as a captive to make proteins that were important for the ancestor cell. Once this happened, all cells that evolved from this ancestor cell had mitochondria, and had the mitochondrial DNA genome too. Mitochondria are inherited from the mother by all offspring—that is, both her female and male offspring. But males are normally mitochondrial "dead ends," and do not pass their mitochondrial DNA to their offspring.

Yep. That's why mtDNA is the tool scientists use to follow females as they moved across the planet.

Making Sense of Male Movement

Remember that humans have 23 pairs of chromosomes. Twenty-two of these pairs are called autosomes (non-sex chromosomes), and most humans have these 22 pairs in most of their cells, whether they are a boy or a girl. Remember, too, that humans have a 23rd pair of chromosomes called the sex chromosome pair. Most girls have two of the same kind of chromosome, called an X chromosome. Most boys have an X chromosome just like girls do, but instead of a second X chromosome boys have what is called a Y chromosome. Females don't have a Y chromosome. So you can actually look at chromosomes from a cell under a microscope, and tell if the cell is from a boy or a girl. The tricky part about these chromosomes is that the Y chromosome is passed on from father to son, making it ideal for tracking male history. So while females are lucky and pass on their mitochondrial DNA, they don't pass on any Y chromosomes because of course they don't have any.

Can you tell which set of chromosomes belongs to a boy and which to a girl?

I can't stand the suspense! What?

They get the Y chromosome from their father, which means it's perfect for following male movement.

Using the Y chromosome, the journey of male humans around the world can be mapped, just like the females were using mtDNA.

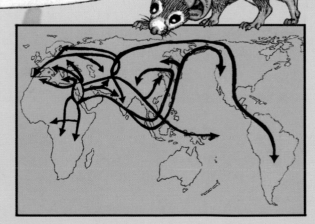

We know where a boy's Y chromosome and a girl's mtDNA come from, but where does the whole boy or the whole girl come from? Let's look at those other 22 pairs of chromosomes—the other 99 percent of the genome.

These other chromosomes get inherited just like the mtDNA and the Y chromosome. So it's going to be easy.

They don't get inherited the same way as the Y chromosome and the mtDNA! The Y chromosome and the mtDNA genome are inherited like clones.

Okay, Darwin. Now you've lost me. Clones?

mtDNA

Y chromosome

1 2 3 4
5 6 7 8
9 10 11 12
13 14 15 16
17 18 19 20
21 22 Y
X

The Other 99% of Your Genome!!

If you are a boy it is possible to get your Y chromosome checked to see which male ancestors gave you the Y chromosome. Everyone can get their mtDNA genome checked to see which female ancestors might have given you that, too. But the rest of your genome is a big jumble of chromosomes. This is because the 22 pairs of autosomes in your genome can recombine with one another. Remember that, for each of your autosome pairs, you get one from your mom and one from your dad.

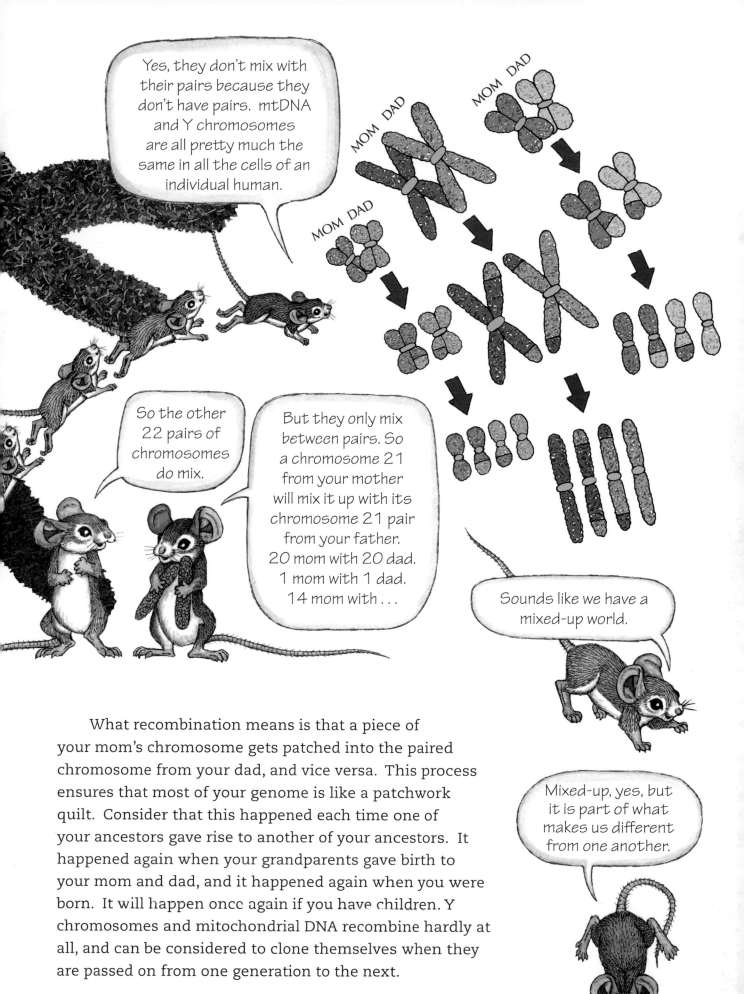

Yes, they don't mix with their pairs because they don't have pairs. mtDNA and Y chromosomes are all pretty much the same in all the cells of an individual human.

So the other 22 pairs of chromosomes do mix.

But they only mix between pairs. So a chromosome 21 from your mother will mix it up with its chromosome 21 pair from your father. 20 mom with 20 dad. 1 mom with 1 dad. 14 mom with . . .

Sounds like we have a mixed-up world.

Mixed-up, yes, but it is part of what makes us different from one another.

What recombination means is that a piece of your mom's chromosome gets patched into the paired chromosome from your dad, and vice versa. This process ensures that most of your genome is like a patchwork quilt. Consider that this happened each time one of your ancestors gave rise to another of your ancestors. It happened again when your grandparents gave birth to your mom and dad, and it happened again when you were born. It will happen once again if you have children. Y chromosomes and mitochondrial DNA recombine hardly at all, and can be considered to clone themselves when they are passed on from one generation to the next.

How *do* we go from mitochondrial genes and Y chromosomal genes, to knowing how and when people moved around the Earth?

Think of genes as a kind of family tree, telling you something about your ancestors.

female male

PEDIGREE CHART

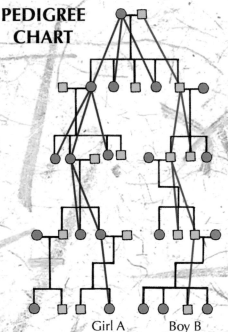

Girl A   Boy B

TREE

Girl A   Boy B

The Pedigree of Women and Men

Pedigrees are simply diagrams of the records of families' births and deaths, and who is born to whom, and who gets married to whom. In pedigree charts, girls are represented by circles, and boys are represented by squares. When a line is drawn between a circle and a square, it means they had children. The children are all drawn below the line linked to the parents. With respect to human movement, two important things can come from a pedigree. A girl can trace her female ancestors back in the pedigree by drawing lines through the circles in the pedigree. A boy can trace his male ancestors back through the pedigree by doing the same thing through the squares. After all of this is done a stick-like diagram, called a tree, is left for how the girls in a family tree are related to one another, and a second one tells how the boys are related to one another. Using DNA to understand our ancestors is exactly like this. Instead of the pedigree giving us a tree, the pattern of changes in DNA gives us a tree, and the tree tells us about our ancestors—male and female—way back in time. But not all genes in our genomes work this way. In fact, there are two major kinds of DNA that scientists have used to look at male and female movement, and these kinds of DNA are the subject of the next pages.

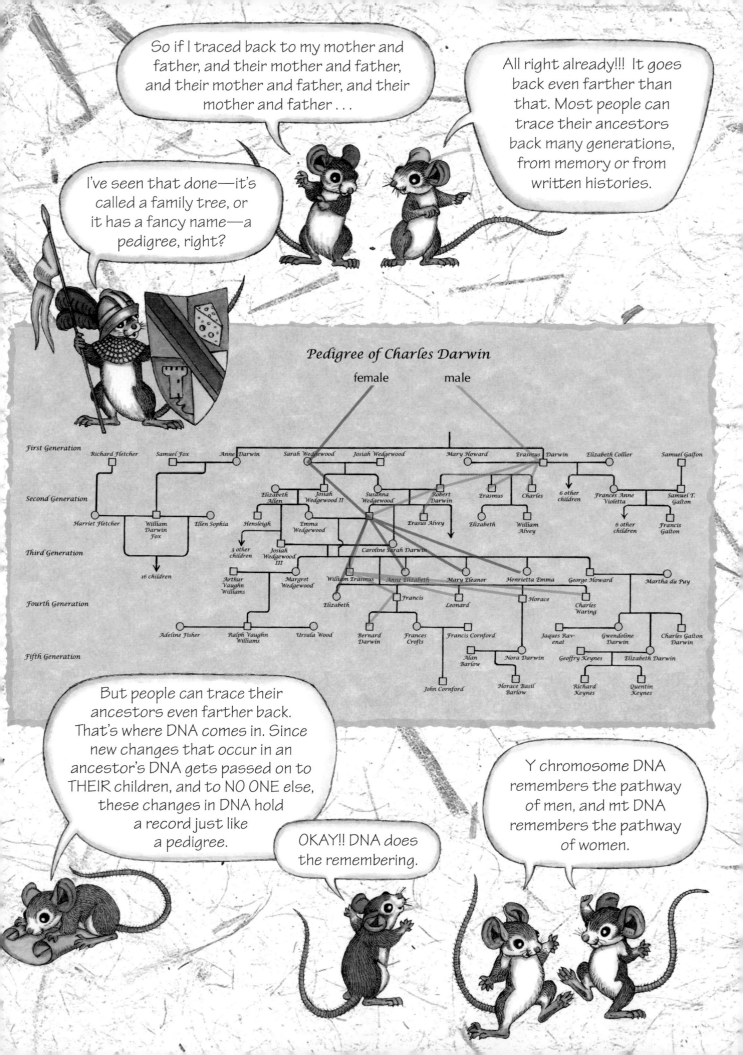

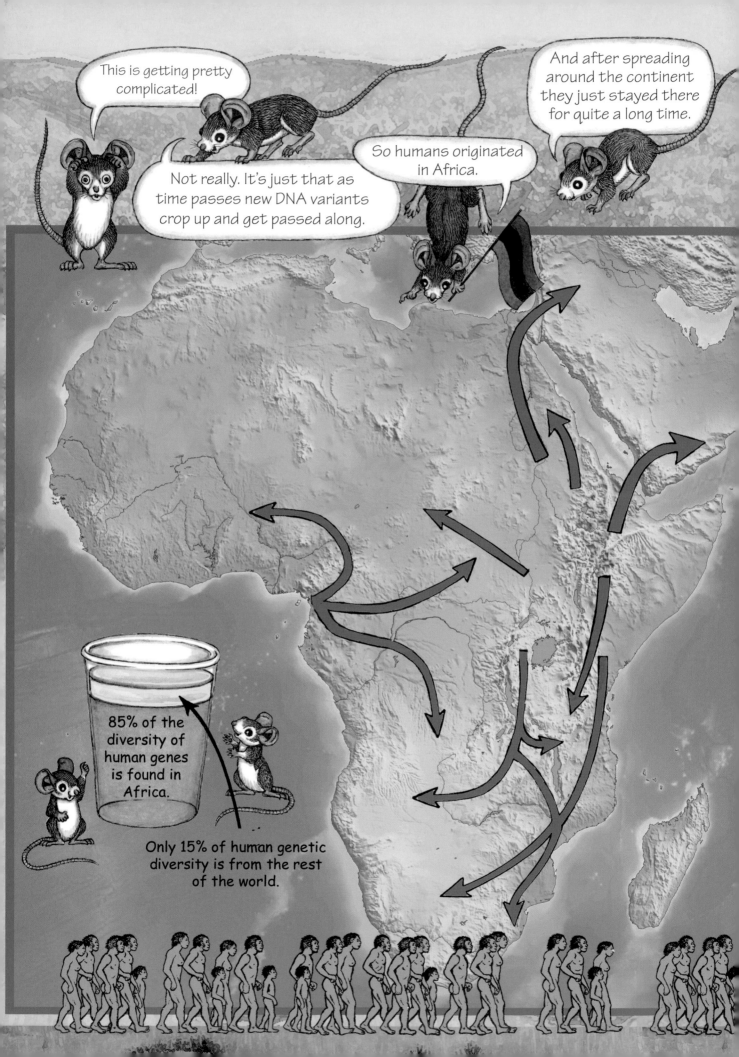

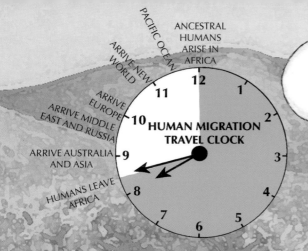

HUMAN MIGRATION TRAVEL CLOCK

ANCESTRAL HUMANS ARISE IN AFRICA

PACIFIC OCEAN
ARRIVE NEW WORLD
ARRIVE EUROPE
ARRIVE MIDDLE EAST AND RUSSIA
ARRIVE AUSTRALIA AND ASIA
HUMANS LEAVE AFRICA

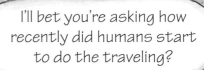

But then they began to leave Africa and spread around the rest of the world.

I'll bet you're asking how recently did humans start to do the traveling?

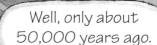

Well, only about 50,000 years ago.

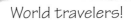

We Are All from Africa (AGAIN AND AGAIN)

If you look at the DNA of people from all over the world—whether that DNA comes from the mitochondrion, or from the Y or other chromosomes—you first of all notice one big thing. This is that in Africa there is more variety than in all the rest of the world put together! And if you look more closely, you notice something else: The variety in the rest of the world is just one part of the African variety. Because DNA variety increases with time, this can mean only one thing. This is that the ancestral humans arose in Africa quite a long time ago—it's believed around 200,000 years—and then one population of these early humans spread out to occupy the rest of the world, probably only about 60,000 thousand years ago. We are all Africans!

Scientists studying mtDNA have traced back the ancestry of the mtDNA of all living people to a single African ancestral mtDNA that they call mitochondrial Eve. Others looking at Y chromosome DNA have identified an African Adam Y chromosome. These are not real people, of course, but particular DNA variants that were present in our ancient ancestors. From the mtDNA ancestor some 18 separate lines of descent have been identified, and from the Y chromosome ancestor 10 lineages have been discovered.

World travelers!

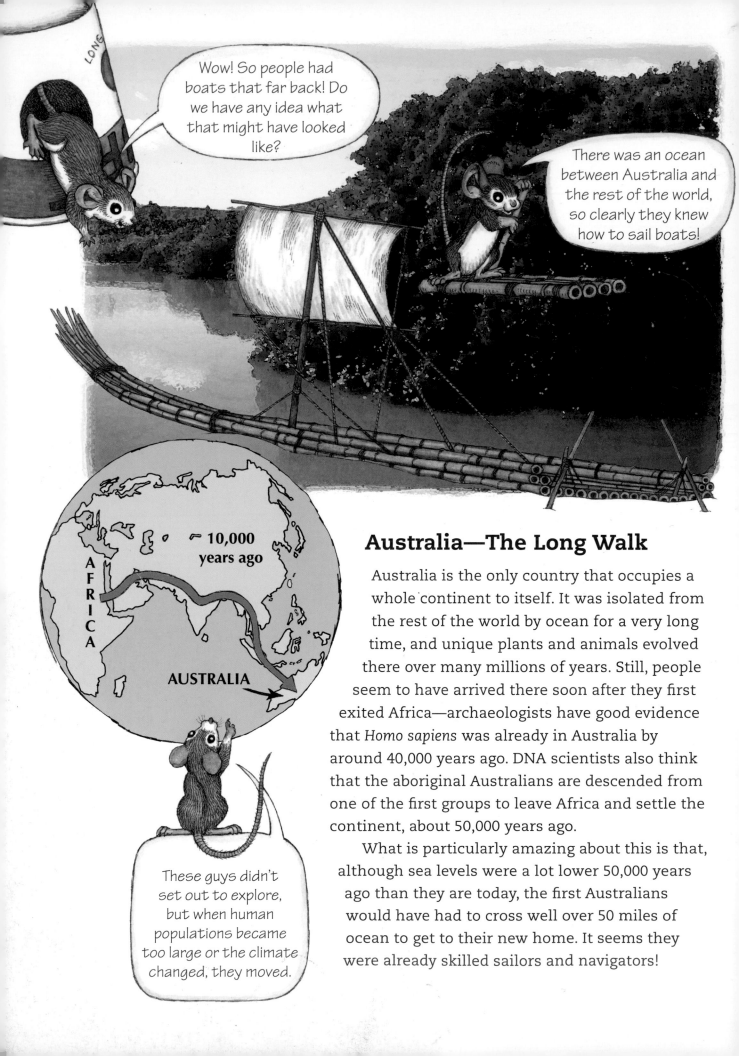

Australia—The Long Walk

Australia is the only country that occupies a whole continent to itself. It was isolated from the rest of the world by ocean for a very long time, and unique plants and animals evolved there over many millions of years. Still, people seem to have arrived there soon after they first exited Africa—archaeologists have good evidence that *Homo sapiens* was already in Australia by around 40,000 years ago. DNA scientists also think that the aboriginal Australians are descended from one of the first groups to leave Africa and settle the continent, about 50,000 years ago.

What is particularly amazing about this is that, although sea levels were a lot lower 50,000 years ago than they are today, the first Australians would have had to cross well over 50 miles of ocean to get to their new home. It seems they were already skilled sailors and navigators!

Humans had never been in Australia before. They must have changed a lot of things.

They sure did. Many native animals became extinct soon after, and most scientists think the early Australians were the cause of their disappearance.

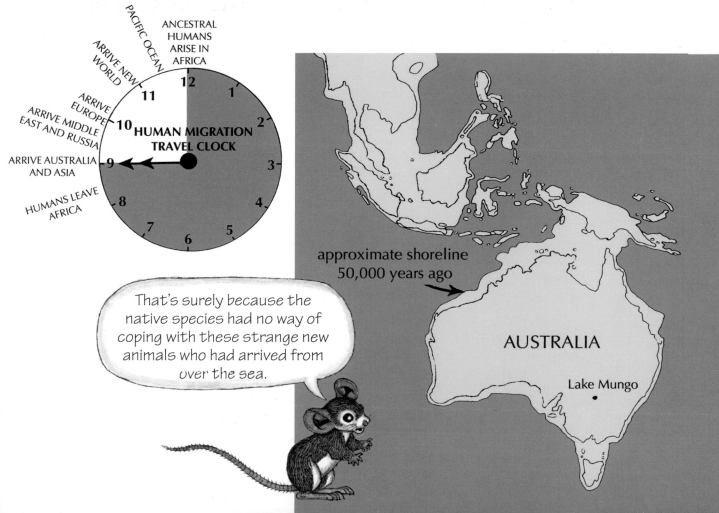

ANCESTRAL HUMANS ARISE IN AFRICA

PACIFIC OCEAN

ARRIVE NEW WORLD

ARRIVE EUROPE

ARRIVE MIDDLE EAST AND RUSSIA

ARRIVE AUSTRALIA AND ASIA

HUMANS LEAVE AFRICA

HUMAN MIGRATION TRAVEL CLOCK

12 1 2 3 4 5 6 7 8 9 10 11

approximate shoreline 50,000 years ago

AUSTRALIA

Lake Mungo

That's surely because the native species had no way of coping with these strange new animals who had arrived from over the sea.

Asia, the Second Stop

Tracing mtDNA and Y chromosomes allows scientists to reconstruct the movements that people have made over the past several thousand years. Both mtDNA and Y chromosomes tell us that there were as many as three major movements of people into the vast continent of Asia, and its island neighbors, during the past 50,000 years. The first migration was into Eastern Asia. The second was into Siberia, and the third was into Asia Minor and the Arabian Peninsula.

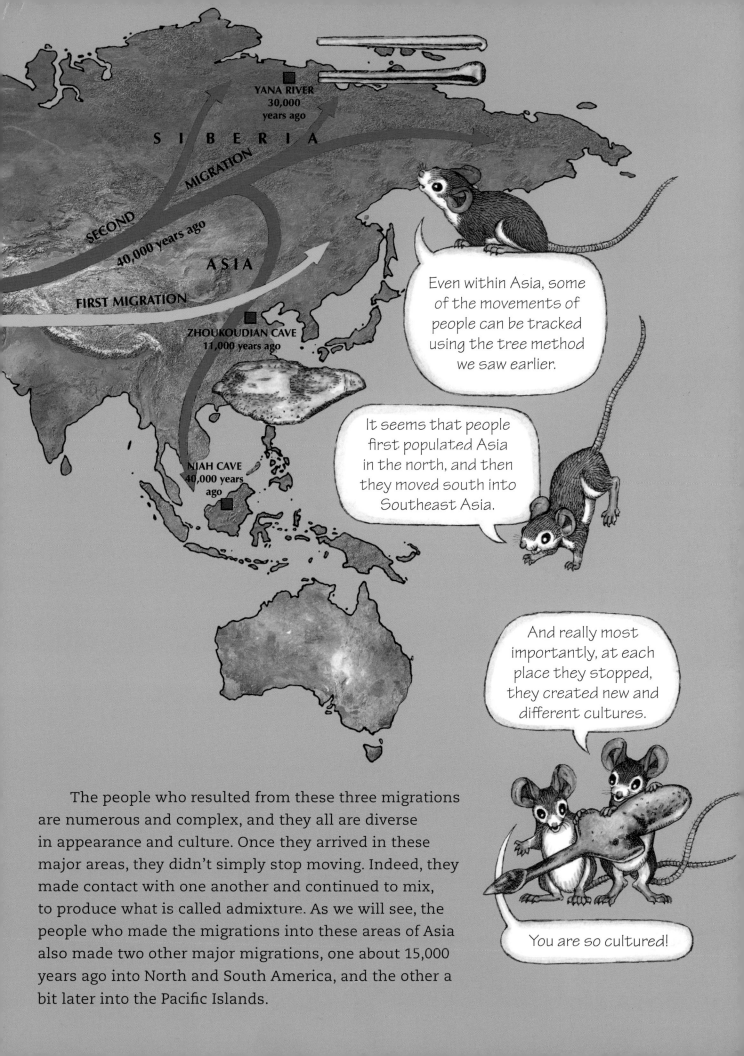

YANA RIVER
30,000
years ago

S I B E R I A

SECOND MIGRATION

40,000 years ago

FIRST MIGRATION

A S I A

ZHOUKOUDIAN CAVE
11,000 years ago

NIAH CAVE
40,000 years ago

Even within Asia, some of the movements of people can be tracked using the tree method we saw earlier.

It seems that people first populated Asia in the north, and then they moved south into Southeast Asia.

And really most importantly, at each place they stopped, they created new and different cultures.

You are so cultured!

The people who resulted from these three migrations are numerous and complex, and they all are diverse in appearance and culture. Once they arrived in these major areas, they didn't simply stop moving. Indeed, they made contact with one another and continued to mix, to produce what is called admixture. As we will see, the people who made the migrations into these areas of Asia also made two other major migrations, one about 15,000 years ago into North and South America, and the other a bit later into the Pacific Islands.

Europe

Human beings got to Europe about 40,000 years ago, arriving from the east after making their way out of Africa perhaps ten thousand years earlier. The early Europeans, often known as Cro-Magnons, left behind a really amazing record of creativity and artistic achievement. They painted powerful animal and geometrical images in caves, they decorated the handles of tools, they played music on bone flutes, and they kept records by engraving on flat plaques of bone and antler. As far as brainpower was concerned, they were just like us.

This is a cute place. Where are we?

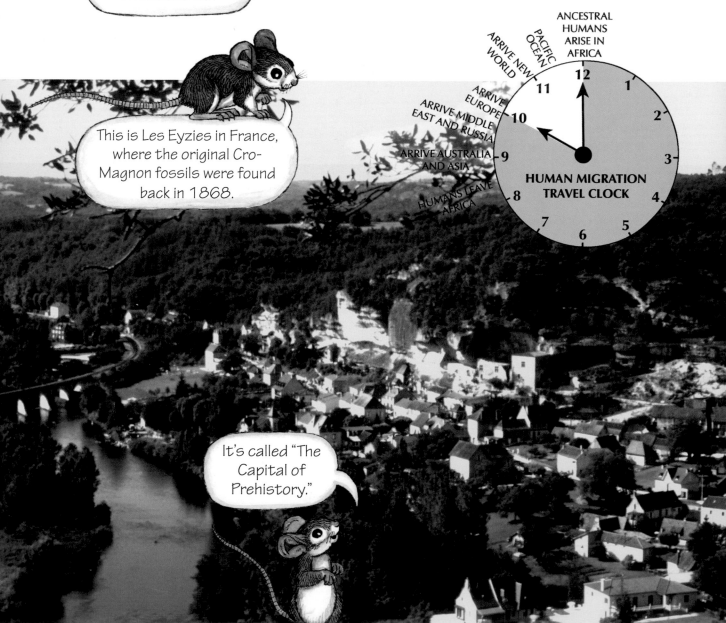

This is Les Eyzies in France, where the original Cro-Magnon fossils were found back in 1868.

It's called "The Capital of Prehistory."

HUMAN MIGRATION TRAVEL CLOCK

ANCESTRAL HUMANS ARISE IN AFRICA

ARRIVE NEW WORLD

PACIFIC OCEAN

ARRIVE EUROPE

ARRIVE MIDDLE EAST AND RUSSIA

ARRIVE AUSTRALIA AND ASIA

HUMANS LEAVE AFRICA

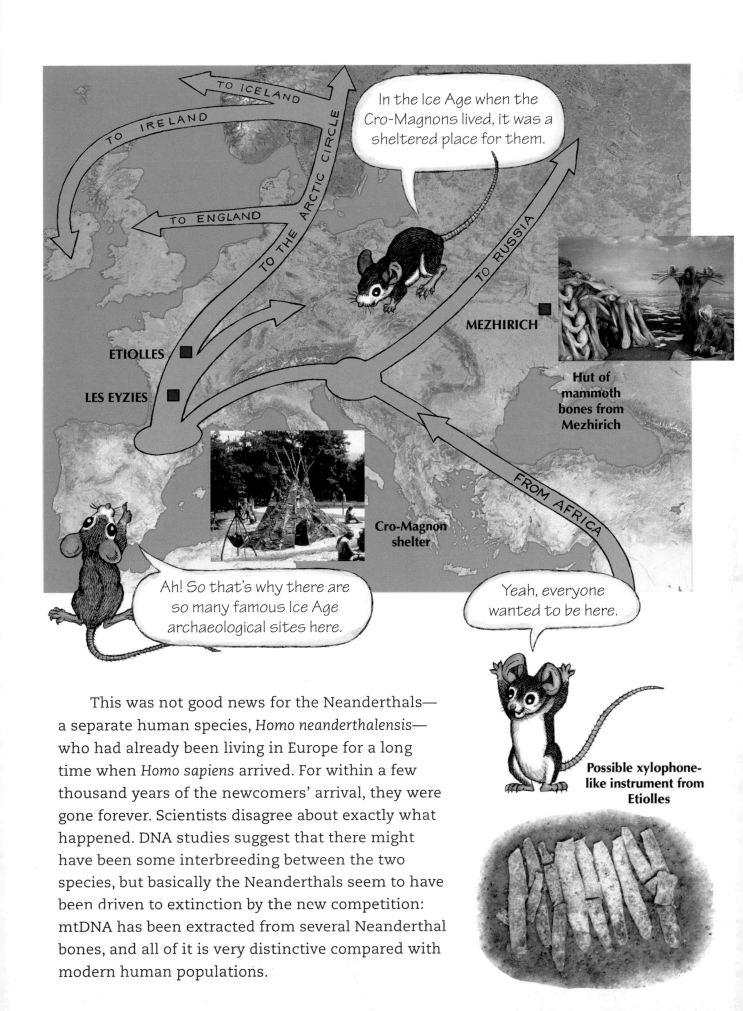

In the Ice Age when the Cro-Magnons lived, it was a sheltered place for them.

Hut of mammoth bones from Mezhirich

Cro-Magnon shelter

Ah! So that's why there are so many famous Ice Age archaeological sites here.

Yeah, everyone wanted to be here.

Possible xylophone-like instrument from Etiolles

This was not good news for the Neanderthals—a separate human species, *Homo neanderthalensis*—who had already been living in Europe for a long time when *Homo sapiens* arrived. For within a few thousand years of the newcomers' arrival, they were gone forever. Scientists disagree about exactly what happened. DNA studies suggest that there might have been some interbreeding between the two species, but basically the Neanderthals seem to have been driven to extinction by the new competition: mtDNA has been extracted from several Neanderthal bones, and all of it is very distinctive compared with modern human populations.

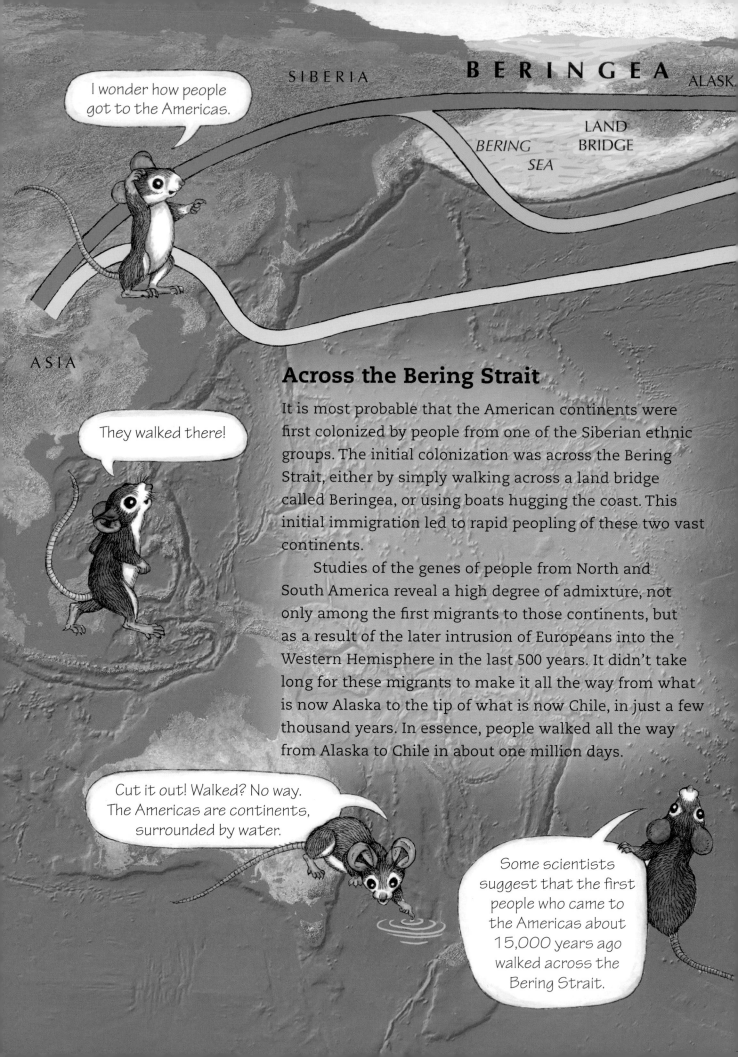

Across the Bering Strait

It is most probable that the American continents were first colonized by people from one of the Siberian ethnic groups. The initial colonization was across the Bering Strait, either by simply walking across a land bridge called Beringea, or using boats hugging the coast. This initial immigration led to rapid peopling of these two vast continents.

Studies of the genes of people from North and South America reveal a high degree of admixture, not only among the first migrants to those continents, but as a result of the later intrusion of Europeans into the Western Hemisphere in the last 500 years. It didn't take long for these migrants to make it all the way from what is now Alaska to the tip of what is now Chile, in just a few thousand years. In essence, people walked all the way from Alaska to Chile in about one million days.

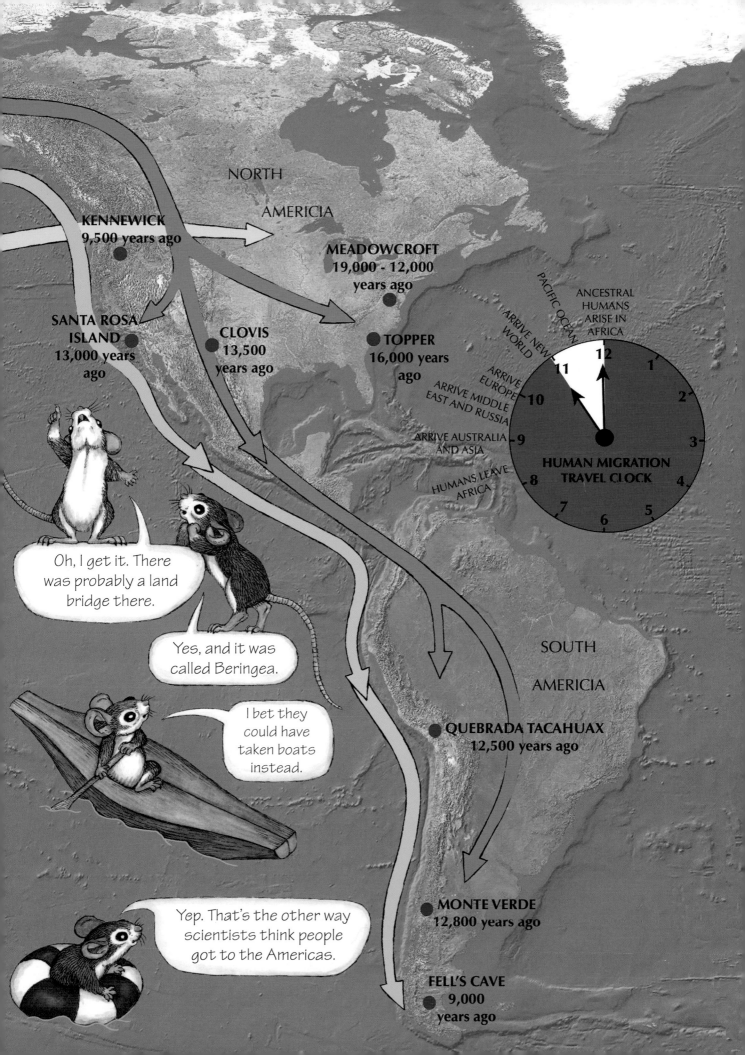

I'm feeling seasick! We've been on the ocean for weeks!

You have to be if you want to reach most of these tiny islands. Imagine if all we had to eat was dried taro root!

I hear our friends the rats have been useful in sorting out who went where and when.

You know the rats! They stowed away in the humans' canoes, and formed their own colonies on new islands. Their descendants' DNA helps confirm the humans' travels.

The Pacific Islands

When Captain Cook explored the Pacific Ocean 250 years ago, he was amazed to find people living on even the most remote islands in this vast body of water. The people who first reached these islands were seafarers of enormous skill and bravery, able to pilot frail canoes over hundreds and even thousands of miles of open sea, in one of the most amazing human achievements of all time. Many lines of evidence, including mtDNA and Y chromosome DNA, have been used to reconstruct the routes by which the islands of the Pacific were colonized.

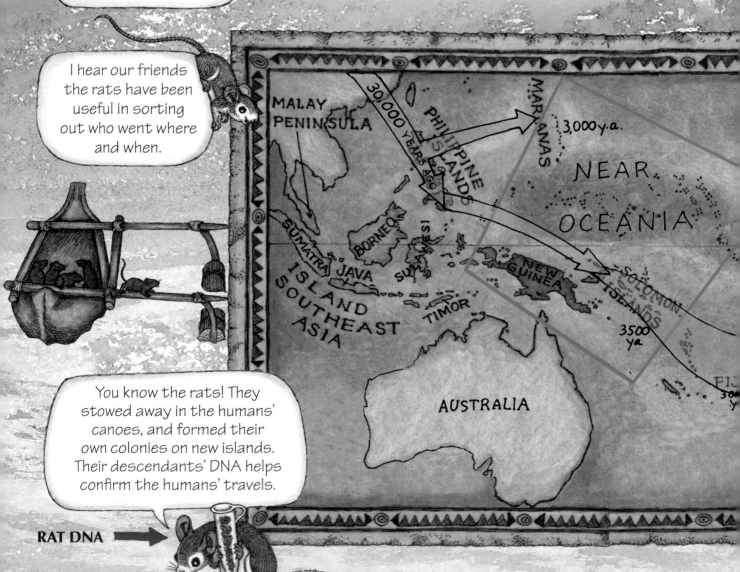

RAT DNA ➤

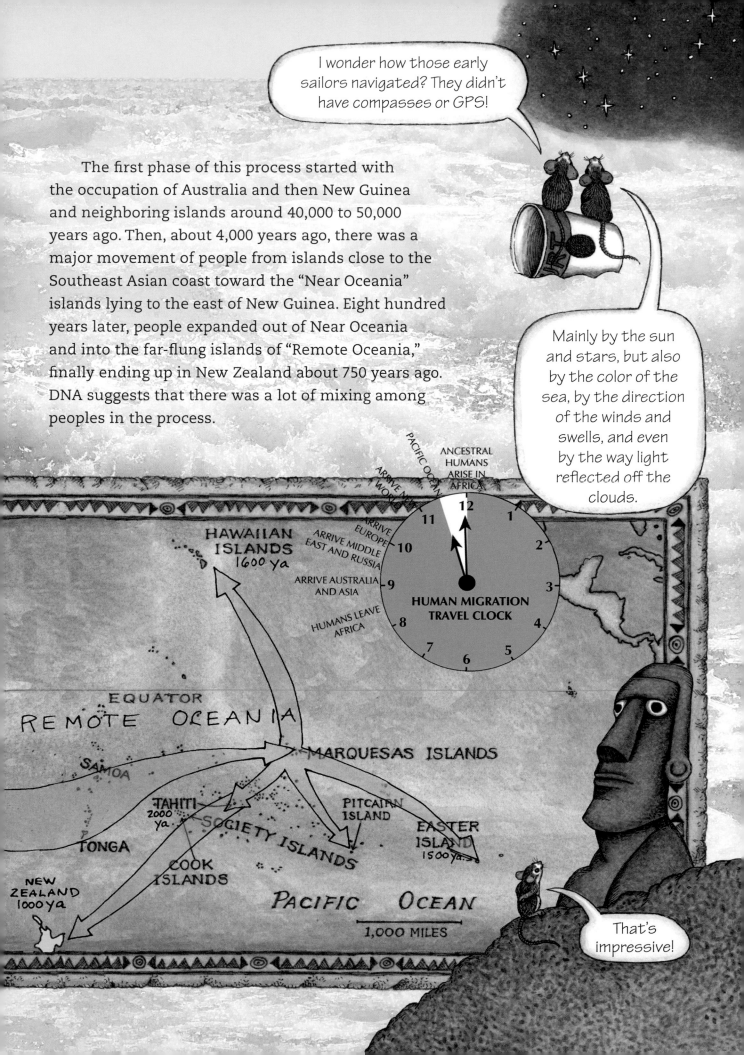

I wonder how those early sailors navigated? They didn't have compasses or GPS!

The first phase of this process started with the occupation of Australia and then New Guinea and neighboring islands around 40,000 to 50,000 years ago. Then, about 4,000 years ago, there was a major movement of people from islands close to the Southeast Asian coast toward the "Near Oceania" islands lying to the east of New Guinea. Eight hundred years later, people expanded out of Near Oceania and into the far-flung islands of "Remote Oceania," finally ending up in New Zealand about 750 years ago. DNA suggests that there was a lot of mixing among peoples in the process.

Mainly by the sun and stars, but also by the color of the sea, by the direction of the winds and swells, and even by the way light reflected off the clouds.

PACIFIC OCEAN

ANCESTRAL HUMANS ARISE IN AFRICA

ARRIVE NEW WORLD

ARRIVE EUROPE

ARRIVE MIDDLE EAST AND RUSSIA

ARRIVE AUSTRALIA AND ASIA

HUMANS LEAVE AFRICA

HUMAN MIGRATION TRAVEL CLOCK

HAWAIIAN ISLANDS 1600 ya

EQUATOR

REMOTE OCEANIA

SAMOA

MARQUESAS ISLANDS

TAHITI 2000 ya

SOCIETY ISLANDS

PITCAIRN ISLAND

EASTER ISLAND 1500 ya

TONGA

COOK ISLANDS

NEW ZEALAND 1000 ya

PACIFIC OCEAN

1,000 MILES

That's impressive!

Mice and Lice

Scientists have discovered that by using the genes of organisms that are parasites of humans, they can reconstruct human history. While viruses aren't organisms, they can be used too. One virus is called human papilloma virus, and causes cervical cancer. It has the same historic pattern as human females. A bacterium called *Helicobacter pylori* that causes ulcers has a very similar history to humans as a whole. Lice, small insect parasites, have histories similar to humans. And mice have been used to trace the history of people living on the Pacific Ocean Islands. How can this be? It's pretty simple, really. These organisms can't live without humans; they either feed off their blood, replicate in their tissues, or feed off their garbage. Since they can't live without humans, they have co-evolved with them. This co-evolution makes their patterns of evolution the same as their human hosts'.

Trains, Planes, and Automobiles

It is about 22 million days since modern humans first left Africa. They didn't set out to go anywhere in particular; instead, populations just expanded and edged gradually into new areas, with a lot of bumps along the way. Individuals probably typically spent their entire lifetimes within a few dozen miles. But even if you are on foot, carrying everything you own, you and your descendants can cover a lot of territory in a few thousand years, exactly as the ancestors of the first Australians did.

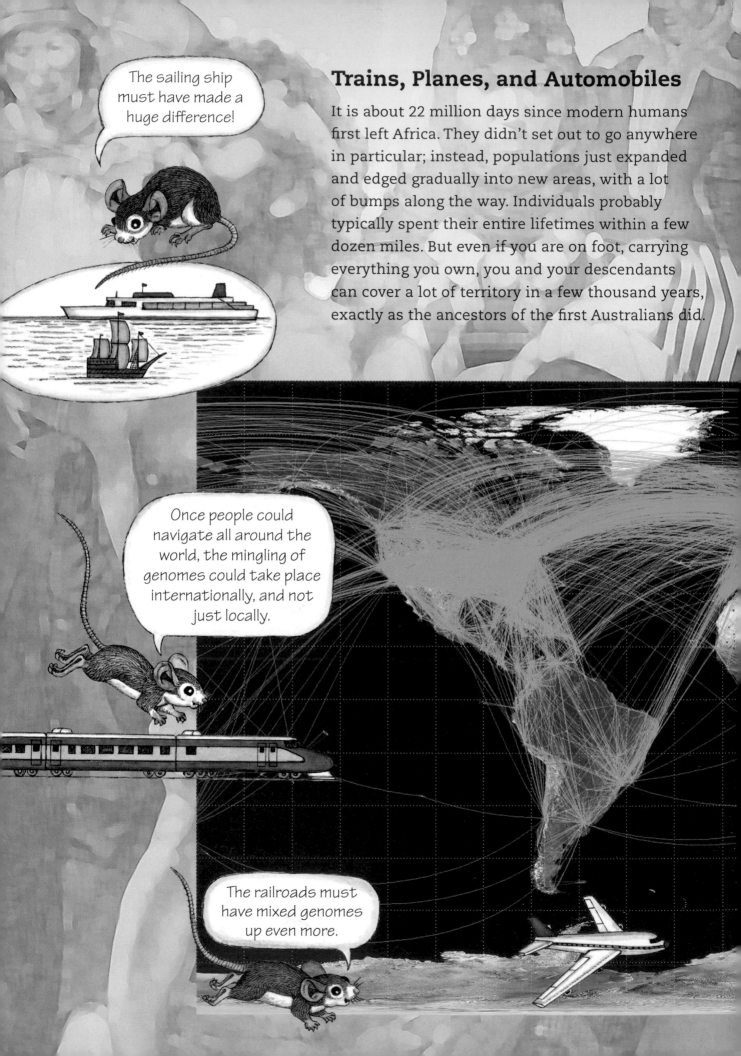

The sailing ship must have made a huge difference!

Once people could navigate all around the world, the mingling of genomes could take place internationally, and not just locally.

The railroads must have mixed genomes up even more.

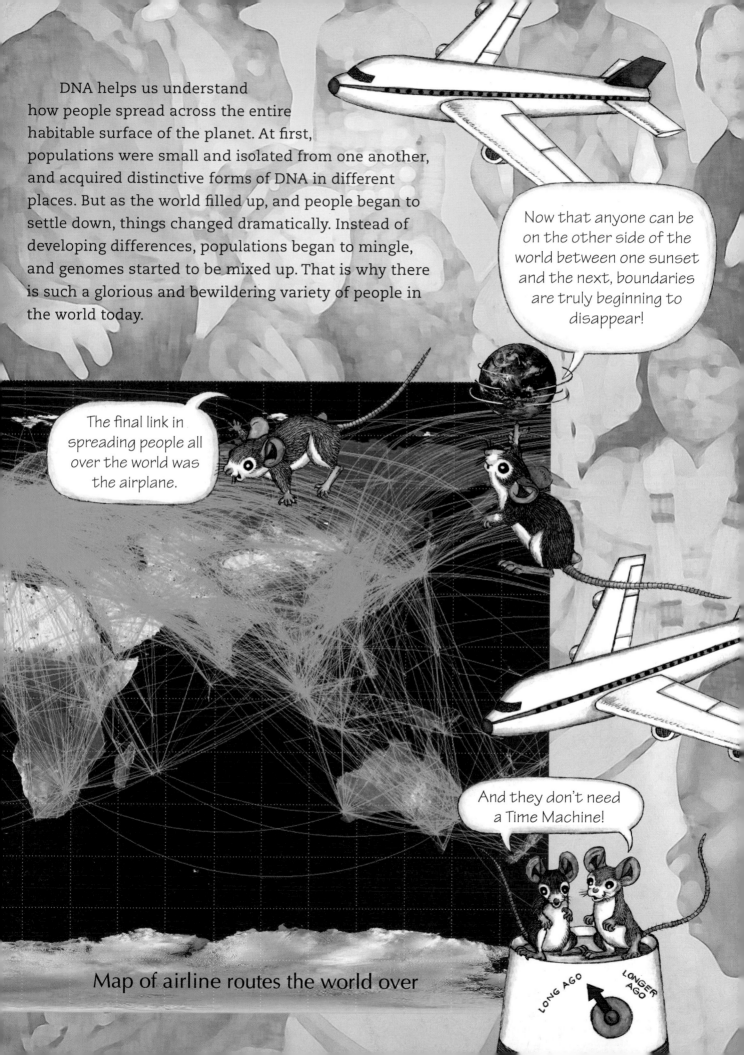

DNA helps us understand how people spread across the entire habitable surface of the planet. At first, populations were small and isolated from one another, and acquired distinctive forms of DNA in different places. But as the world filled up, and people began to settle down, things changed dramatically. Instead of developing differences, populations began to mingle, and genomes started to be mixed up. That is why there is such a glorious and bewildering variety of people in the world today.

Now that anyone can be on the other side of the world between one sunset and the next, boundaries are truly beginning to disappear!

The final link in spreading people all over the world was the airplane.

And they don't need a Time Machine!

LONG AGO   LONGER AGO

Map of airline routes the world over

Hey Wallace, this trip around the world has been fun and we saw some cool things. Where do you want to go now?

How do you like climbing trees??

Fun!! Which tree are we talking about?

Why, the great tree of life, the tree that describes the relationships among all life-forms on this planet!!

Let's do it!!

www.bunkerhillpublishing.com
by Bunker Hill Publishing Inc., 285 River Road, Piermont, New Hampshire 03779, USA

10 9 8 7 6 5 4 3 2 1

Library of Congress Control Number: 2013934780

ISBN 978-1-59373-148-9

Designed by Joe Lops
Printed in China

Image Credits: Pp. 2, 3, 4, 5, 6, 8, 9, 15 AMNH;
pp. 1, 6, 7 Willard Whitson; pp. 38, 39 Ian Tattersall; pp. 8, 9 Chenshilwood at en.wikipedia;
p. 10 Dragi Markovic; pp. 32, 39, 40, 41, 44 USGS; p. 39 Yvette Taborin;
all other images, Patricia J. Wynne